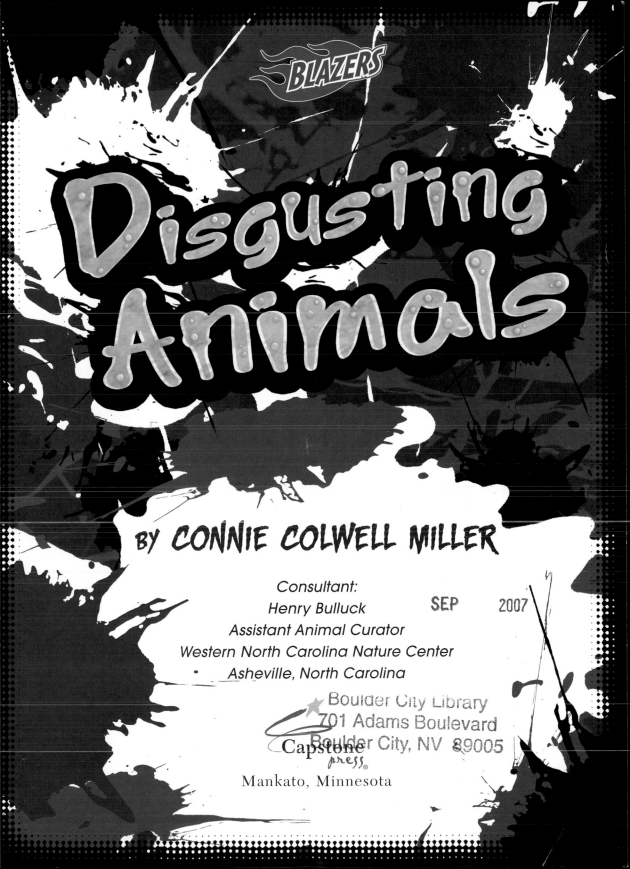

BLAZERS

# Disgusting Animals

BY CONNIE COLWELL MILLER

Consultant:
Henry Bulluck
Assistant Animal Curator
Western North Carolina Nature Center
Asheville, North Carolina

Capstone
press®

Mankato, Minnesota

Blazers Books are published by Capstone Press,
151 Good Counsel Drive, P.O. Box 669, Mankato, Minnesota 56002.
www.capstonepress.com

*Library of Congress Cataloging-in-Publication Data*
Miller, Connie Colwell, 1976–
    Disgusting animals / by Connie Colwell Miller.
    p. cm.—(Blazers. That's disgusting!)
    Includes bibliographical references and index.
    ISBN-13: 978-0-7368-6797-9 (hardcover)
    ISBN-10: 0-7368-6797-X (hardcover)
    ISBN-13: 978-0-7368-7875-3 (softcover pbk.)
    ISBN-10: 0-7368-7875-0 (softcover pbk.)
    1. Animal behavior—Juvenile literature. 2. Animal defenses—Juvenile literature.
I. Title. II. Series.
QL751.5.M55 2007
591.5—dc22                                                    2006026400

Summary: Describes 10 disgusting animals and what makes them gross.

**Editorial Credits**
Mandy Robbins, editor; Thomas Emery, designer; Bob Lentz, illustrator;
    Jo Miller, photo researcher/photo editor

**Photo Credits**
Ardea/John Cancalosi, 12–13; Pat Morris, 22–23
Corbis/Brandon D. Cole, 23 (inset); DK Limited, 11 (inset);
    Joe McDonald, 11, 18–19; zefa/Daniel Boschung, 28–29
Grant Heilman Photography/Peter Dean, 6–7
Index Stock Imagery/Tom Carroll, 14–15
McDonald Wildlife Photography/Joe McDonald, 20–21
Minden Pictures/Cyril Ruoso/JH Editorial, 26–27
Nature Picture Library/ARCO/De Meester, 4–5; Jim Clare, 24–25;
    Simon Wagen/J. Downer Product, 8–9
Photo Researchers Inc./Jeffrey Lepore, 16–17
Shutterstock/javarman, cover

1 2 3 4 5 6 12 11 10 09 08 07

# Table of Contents

# That's Disgusting!

Cats lick their rear ends. Seems pretty gross to humans, but it's how cats keep clean.

Most people enjoy watching animals. But don't get too close! Animals have some nasty habits.

## GROSS-O-METER

Use this meter to gauge how disgusting these animals really are.

THAT'S DISGUSTING

# Chew On This

After eating, cattle cough up their food and chew it again. The chewed-up food is called cud. Chewing cud helps cattle digest their food.

SORT OF DISGUSTING

GROSS-O-METER

**BLAZER FACT**

Cattle chew their cud for up to eight hours a day.

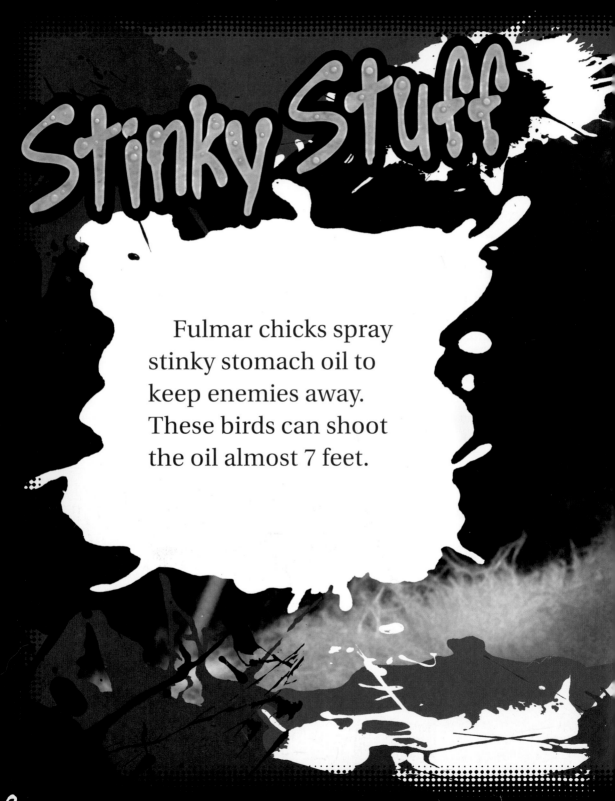

# Stinky Stuff

Fulmar chicks spray stinky stomach oil to keep enemies away. These birds can shoot the oil almost 7 feet.

GROSS-O-METER

SORT OF DISGUSTING

# Bird Barf

Owls swallow mice, birds, and insects whole. After eating, they throw up pellets of fur, bones, teeth, and feathers.

GROSS-O-METER

SORT OF DISGUSTING

*Owl pellet*

# Blood Bath

A frightened horned lizard will shoot blood from its eyes. The blood distracts enemies and gives the lizard a chance to get away.

GROSS-O-METER

SORT OF DISGUSTING

## BLAZER FACT

Horned lizards can squirt blood as far as 4 feet.

# Green and Gross

Llamas spit at each other to guard their meals. They can spew smelly green goo up to 15 feet.

GROSS-O-METER

PRETTY DISGUSTING

Llama slobber smells so bad, it makes other llamas lose their appetites.

# Stink Out

Scaring a skunk can have lasting effects. A frightened skunk will spray a stinky mist out of its behind. The smell can stick around for two years!

## GROSS-O-METER

PRETTY DISGUSTING

# Playing Dead

Opossums make enemies think they are already dead. A scared opossum rolls onto its side and sticks out its tongue. Then it poops on itself.

GROSS-O-METER

PRETTY DISGUSTING

# Rotting Flesh

Black widow spiders shoot poison into their prey. The poison rots the animal's insides. Then the spider sucks them out.

GROSS-O-METER

PRETTY DISGUSTING

# Slime Time

GROSS-O-METER

REALLY DISGUSTING

Hagfish are long, slimy fish with nasty eating habits. A hagfish will squeeze inside a dead animal and eat its way out.

*Hagfish baring its teeth*

# Blood Suckers

Vampire bats drink the blood of cattle, horses, and pigs. Their spit keeps the animal's blood flowing until the bat is full.

GROSS-O-METER

REALLY DISGUSTING

## BLAZER FACT

A vampire bat's spit numbs its victim's skin, so the animal can't feel the bite.

# The Bite That Kills

GROSS-O-METER

REALLY DISGUSTING

The komodo dragon's mouth is so dirty, just one bite is deadly. The germs in its saliva can kill almost any animal—even people.

# Dirty Behavior

Pigs eat almost anything, including cattle poop. And humans eat pigs!

Animals throw up. They spit. They spray stuff out of their behinds. But all of these disgusting behaviors help animals survive.

We made it through, and I have one thing to say. **That's disgusting!**

# Glossary

**cud** (KUHD)—food that has not been digested that cows bring up to chew again

**digest** (dye-JEST)—to break down food so that it can be used by the body

**enemy** (EN-uh-mee)—an animal that wants to harm or kill another animal

**fulmar** (FUHL-mahr)—a bird similar to a sea gull that lives in very cold regions of the world

**germ** (JURM)—a very small living organism that can cause disease

**pellet** (PEL-it)—a mass of undigested hair, fur, and bones vomited by an owl

**prey** (PRAY)—an animal that is hunted by another animal for food

**saliva** (suh-LYE-vuh)—the clear liquid in the mouth

# Read More

**Murphy, Patricia J.** *Why Do Some Animals Shed Their Skin?* The Library of Why. New York: PowerKids Press, 2004.

**Branzei, Sylvia.** *Animal Grossology: The Science of Creatures Gross and Disgusting.* New York: Penguin Young Readers Group, 2004.

**Szpirglas, Jeff.** *Gross Universe: Your Guide to All Disgusting Things Under the Sun.* Toronto: Maple Tree Press, 2004.

# Internet Sites

FactHound offers a safe, fun way to find Internet sites related to this book. All of the sites on FactHound have been researched by our staff.

Here's how:

1. Visit *www.facthound.com*

2. Choose your grade level.

3. Type in this book ID **073686797X** for age-appropriate sites. You may also browse subjects by clicking on letters, or by clicking on pictures and words.

4. Click on the **Fetch It** button.

**FactHound will fetch the best sites for you!**

# Index